FUN & GAMES

For Gerrit

PHOTO CREDITS

Astronauts: NASA, pages 4–5; bouncing ball: C. E. Miller/MIT, pages 6–7; leaping gymnast: Bruce Curtis/Peter Arnold, Inc., pages 8–9; foot and football: C. E. Miller/MIT, pages 10–11; tennis ball and racket: C. E. Miller/MIT, pages 12–13; karate chop: C. E. Miller/MIT, pages 14–15; hands of piano player and banjo picker: Howard Sochurek, pages 3, 16–17; needle and tonearm head: June T. Hull/Clairol, Inc., pages 18–19; audioscope: Manfred Kage/Peter Arnold, Inc., pages 20–21; running shoes and soles of feet: Inframetrics/Nike, pages 22–23; Vail, Colorado: NASA, pages 24–25; popcorn popping: Greg and Bruce Dale, pages 26–27; brain during language and music stimulation: Anza/Peter Arnold, Inc., pages 28–29; electrical field from fingertip: Astrid & Frieder Michler/Peter Arnold, Inc., page 30.

First Edition 1 2 3 4 5 6 7 8 9 10

Library of Congress Cataloging in Publication Data
Cobb, Vicki. Fun & games : stories science photos tell / by Vicki Cobb.   p.   cm. Summary: Examines in text and special, detailed photographs how popcorn pops, how a ball bounces, how a phonograph needle "reads" the sound on a record, what happens in the brain when one is listening to words and music, and many other things. ISBN 0-688-09315-9.—ISBN 0-688-09316-7 (lib. bdg.) 1. Science—Experiments—Juvenile literature. 2. Scientific recreations—Juvenile literature. [1. Science—Miscellanea. 2. Scientific recreations.] I. Title. II. Title: Fun and games. Q164.C485 1992 507.8—dc20 90-22792 CIP AC

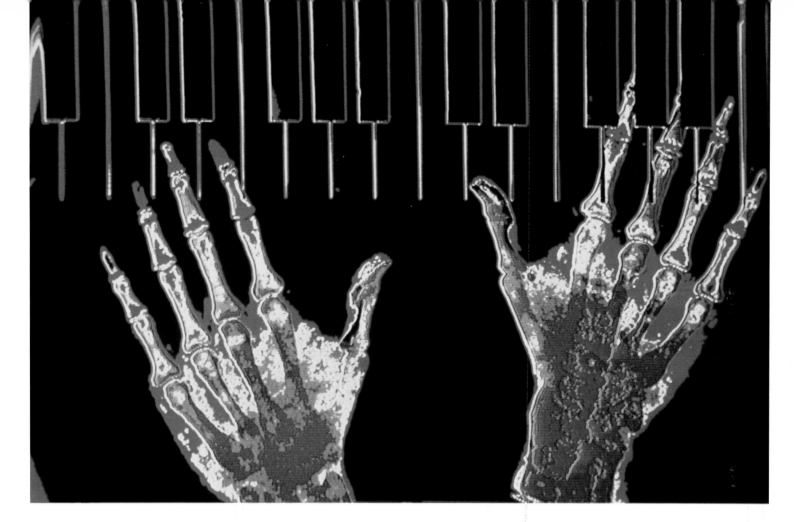

FUN & GAMES

STORIES SCIENCE PHOTOS TELL

BY VICKI COBB

LOTHROP, LEE & SHEPARD BOOKS   NEW YORK

WHAT'S UP?

Suppose you were suddenly free of the pull of earth's gravity. Naturally, you'd experiment. Maybe you'd try resting in midair or bouncing off the walls. You might close your eyes and try to figure out which way is up. Astronauts are the only people who experience zero gravity long enough to experiment with it. Most of the time during a mission, they are very busy working or taking care of their needs for food and rest. They have only a few moments of leisure. What do they do with them? They do what most people would do with free time—they play.

This picture was taken aboard the space shuttle *Discovery*. *Discovery* was built with a floor and a ceiling to help the astronauts adjust to living where there is no feeling of being up or down. Astronauts Jeffrey Hoffman and Rhea Seddon look as if they are doing the impossible: playing with a slinky while Jeff walks up the wall. The slinky is not sagging, as it would on earth. It looks as if they are defying gravity, but there is no gravity in space. The picture would be just as accurate if you held it sideways or turned it upside down. What's up in this picture? You decide.

People spend leisure time doing things they enjoy. It's interesting to see what scientific photographs reveal about fun and games. They show some surprising and different ways to look at the pastimes that add pleasure to our lives.

A BOUNCING BALL

In many sports, how well you play depends on how well you judge the motion of a ball. Fortunately, the way a ball moves is very predictable. The path of a ball depends on *gravity* and on the strength and direction of the force that sets the ball in motion. With experience, skilled athletes can make balls go where they want them to go and quickly get into position to meet moving balls.

This multiple-exposure photograph of a bouncing ball was taken in the dark with the camera shutter open. It is safe to leave the shutter open when taking pictures in the dark because the film is not exposed unless there is light. In this case, the light came from a high-speed flashing light called a stroboscope, or strobe, which was set to flash at equal *intervals* thirty times per second. The film captured an image of the moving ball each time the strobe flashed. Here are some of the things the photo shows.

The ball is moving fastest where the images are farthest apart and slowest where they are closest together. The changing speed of the ball is the direct result of gravity. When the ball is falling, that is, moving toward the center of the earth, it speeds up. After it bounces and moves away from the pull of gravity, it slows down at exactly the same rate. The ball is moving slowest at the top of the arc and fastest as it hits the ground. After a collision between the ball and the ground, some of the energy in the ball's bounce is lost. A small amount of the energy is absorbed by the ground and some by the ball itself. That's why each bounce loses *altitude*. If the bounce were perfect, no energy would be lost on impact: every bounce would be exactly as high as the last, and the ball would bounce forever. But, of course, the perfect bounce doesn't exist in the real world.

The shape of the ball's path is an open curve called a parabola.

(A circle is a closed curve.) It is the result of the horizontal motion of the ball when it rolled off the ledge and the downward vertical motion caused by gravity. Parabolas can have many different shapes, from tall and skinny to long and low. When you look at the path of a bouncing ball from the side, you can easily see its parabolic shape.

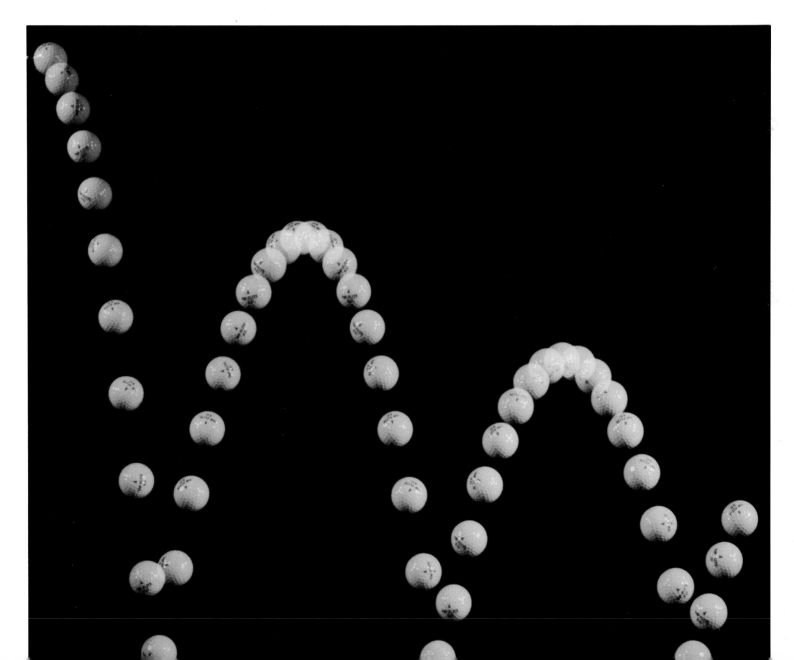

FALLING BODIES

During many recreational activities, the human body is briefly in the air. Since the human body has a shape that is very different from that of a ball, it is harder to see how gravity and other forces shape its path.

Gravity acts on a falling body as if all of the body's weight is in one spot, not spread out as it actually is. This spot is called the center of gravity. A ball is perfectly symmetrical and its matter is evenly distributed throughout, so its center of gravity is also its actual center. If an object has an irregular shape and if it is made up of different kinds of matter, its center of gravity may not be the same as its center. Your body is definitely irregular in shape and is composed of different kinds of matter. When you are standing, your center of gravity is about one inch below your navel. When you fall freely, your center of gravity moves toward the center of the earth in a straight line. If you are tumbling or twisting as you fall, your body rotates around your center of gravity and its straight-line fall. When you leap, your body has two forces operating on it: the forward and upward thrust of your legs and arms, and the downward pull of gravity. These forces combine to determine your path through the air.

The multiple-exposure strobe photo of a leaping gymnast shows how the positions of the arms and legs change during the leap. But the center of gravity—the hips and buttocks of the gymnast—makes a parabolic arc, just the way the bouncing ball did in the preceding photo.

8

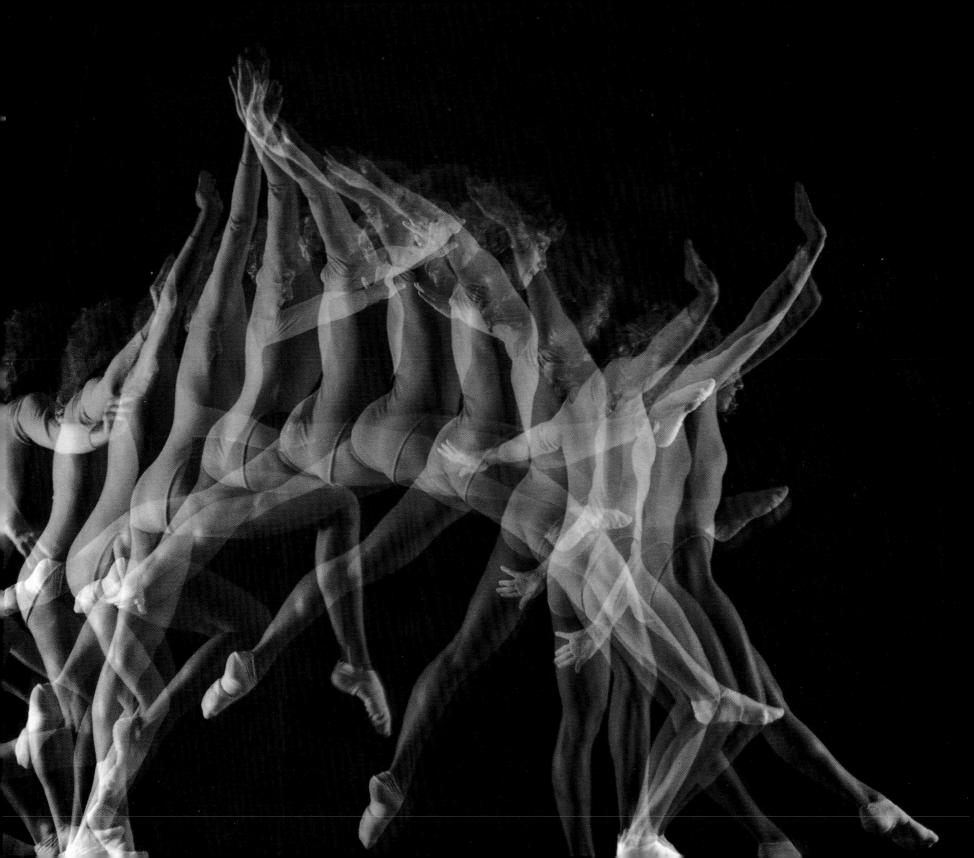

KICKOFF

The object of a football kickoff is to put the ball in motion. Its flight has to be long enough to push the opposing team back in its own territory to catch the ball, and high enough to give the kicking team time to get downfield. When you watch a kickoff, you see the kick and you see the ball fly into the air. You assume that the kicker's foot collides with the ball—the collision itself is too brief for you to see.

This photograph was made with a high-speed strobe. It captures the exact split second when the foot meets the ball, before the ball starts to move away. Now you can see what happens at the moment of impact. You can see that the foot distorts the shape of the football. Some of the energy with which the football leaves the foot comes from the force of the football springing back into shape.

Sir Isaac Newton stated a law of motion that every football kicker knows intuitively: The motion of an object depends on the direction of the force that causes it, the strength of that force, and the time during which it acts.

The foot is traveling at about fifty-five miles an hour when it meets the football. It stays in contact with the ball for .008 seconds. If the foot passes through the ball's center of gravity, the ball will sail through the air without rotating and have the least amount of air resistance. Air resistance is friction from moving air, which slows down objects traveling through it. The best kicks travel sixty yards or more downfield and have a hang time (time in the air) of about four seconds. If the kick is off center, the ball will tumble end over end in the air. This increases air resistance, and the ball does not travel as far. A tumbling football has the advantage, to the kicker's team, of being difficult to catch and unpredictable in its bounce. (For you football buffs, it is used for the onside kick.)

TENNIS BALL AND RACKET

This high-speed strobe photo shows what happens during a collision between a tennis ball and a racket. The impact of the collision, which lasts .005 seconds, flattens the ball, stretches the strings of the racket, and even distorts the frame. If these objects kept their distorted shapes, most of the force of the collision would be absorbed. But they are elastic—they restore themselves to their original shapes after the collision. This is known as having restoring force. When the strings and the ball spring back into shape, their restoring force helps propel the ball, or move it away from the racket. The ideal racket frame would also propel the ball with its restoring force. The frame, however, does not snap back quickly enough to do this, so it absorbs some energy on impact. Tennis-racket designers solve this problem by making stiffer frames. Stiff frames don't add force to the ball, but they absorb less energy than flexible frames do during the collision. Tennis players find that using a stiff racket adds power to their strokes; however, it gives them less control over the placement of the ball.

Strobes can be used to clock the speed of a tennis ball as it leaves the racket. The fastest serve has a speed of more than 130 miles per hour. During the serve, the ball is thrown straight up. It is not moving toward or away from the net. The forward motion of the racket and the restoring forces of the ball and the strings propel the ball. During play, when the ball and racket collide, the racket not only stops the ball but reverses its motion. In a well-hit forehand, the ball travels at a speed of 70 miles per hour.

KARATE CHOP

Karate is a sport in which blows are delivered with an open hand rather than a fist. In fact, the word *karate* means "open hand." This picture shows astronaut Ron McNair, who perished in the *Challenger 7* disaster, breaking a concrete block. The ability of a human hand to deliver such a powerful blow seems super-human. As a black-belt karate expert, Ron made physics and athletic skill work together to produce a force that is well within the range of anyone with normal physical strength.

The force of the blow depends on two things: the *mass* of the hand, and its speed at the moment of impact. Ron's hand makes contact when it reaches its maximum speed, about 30 miles per hour. His wrist and elbow are locked. The power comes from the motion of his upper body and shoulder, not just his arm, so some of his body weight is behind the blow. Scientists calculate that the force delivered by the hand is about 850 pounds and lasts between .005 and .01 seconds. A force of about 650 pounds is required to crack a concrete slab 1½ inches thick. After the hand strikes the concrete, it slows down very quickly and it, too, experiences a force. Concrete is not a flexible material. If it receives enough force to bend it only .025 inches, it will break. A human hand can withstand much greater compression without injury than the concrete. You can feel this by using one hand to squeeze together the sides of your other hand much more than a fortieth of an inch.

As long as the concrete breaks, the moment or so of compression does not damage the hand. But if the blow doesn't break the concrete, the hand can be injured. Ouch!

PRACTICING HANDS

If you practice any physical activity long enough, two things happen: You get good at the activity, and your muscles and bones change to reflect your efforts. These scientific photographs show the hands of two musicians who have been playing their instruments daily for more than twenty years. One is a piano player and the other is a banjo picker. The shape of these people's hands undoubtedly differed to begin with, but the photos show how years of practice have affected the shapes of the bones of the fingers and the muscles of the hands. The piano player uses his hands as a hammer, pounding away at the keys. His hands are compact, his fingers are thick, and his palms are strong. The banjo picker plucks the strings with his fingers. His fingers are tapered,

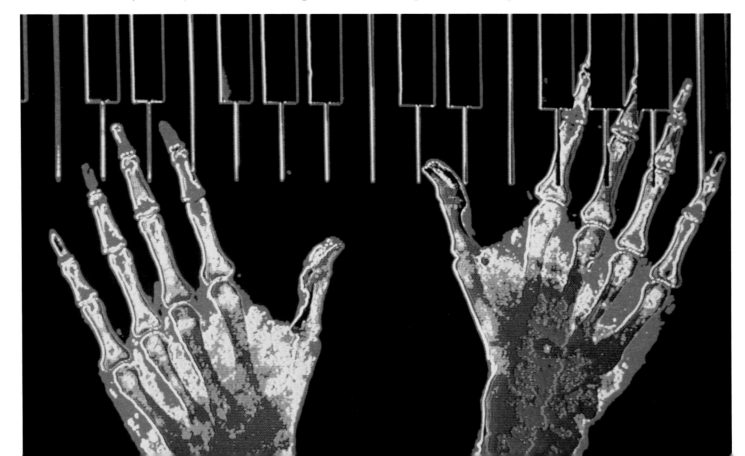

and there is not as much muscle in the palm of his hand. The end joints of his fingers are still flexible.

These photographs began as X rays, which show bone and muscle as gray shadows. The fifteen or sixteen shades of gray in an X ray are not easily distinguishable by the human eye. The X rays were scanned by a laser beam that put all the different shades of gray into a computer. The computer could then be used to give each shade of gray a different signal. The images were finely focused, all fuzziness was eliminated, and colors were added to enhance the differences between bone and muscle. The colors were decided by the technician who did the work; there is no standard color for bone or for muscle. This process is called *computer enhancement*. These days, a great deal of medical diagnosis depends on computer enhancement of X rays.

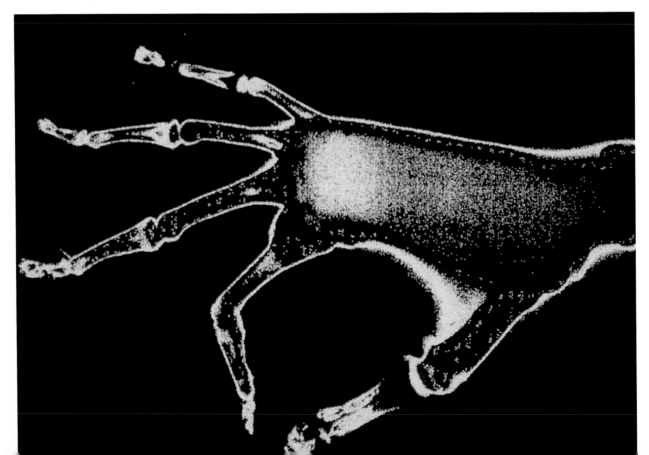

PHONOGRAPH NEEDLE AND RECORD

Sound is the sensation produced by vibrations that reach our ears. A group of many random sounds or tones is called noise; music is organized sound made up of many tones. People spend many happy hours listening to music that has been preserved by modern inventions such as records. The music on a phonograph record is captured in a spiral groove carved into a plastic disc. The phonograph needle rests lightly in the groove. As the record turns, the zigzag shape of the groove causes the needle to vibrate from side to side. These vibrations go from the needle to the *tonearm*, where they are transformed into electrical signals. When the signals are amplified, or made louder, you hear these vibrations as music. The original music was recorded in a reverse process. A microphone transformed the music into electrical signals. These signals went through a recording arm that caused a very sharp needle to vibrate back and forth on a spinning disc. The needle carved a groove in this master record, from which other records were made.

This photograph of a phonograph needle in the groove of a record was made with a scanning electron microscope. A beam of electrons scans the subject by moving back and forth over it. An enlarged image of the subject appears on a television screen. A photograph of the image made with a scanning electron microscope is called a scanning electron micrograph, or SEM for short. This SEM shows segments of the spiral groove of a record. You can see that the channel of the groove has an irregular pattern, which is caused by the variety of sounds in the music. The rounded bottom of the needle prevents it from touching the bottom of the groove and the tonearm is *counterbalanced*, so that the needle's motion is almost without friction that might interfere with the *fidelity* of the sound.

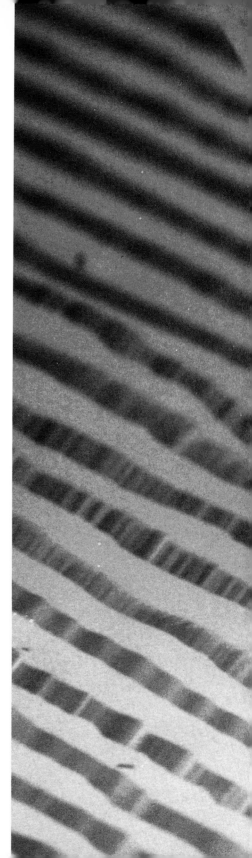

Two beautiful notes

If you could see sound, what would it look like? Set a bell ringing and put its edge in water. See the waves it generates on the surface of the water. Most of the sounds you hear are complicated because they are made up of many different sound waves. Scientists try to simplify complicated things. The simplest sound is a tone. By understanding individual tones, scientists build a foundation for understanding more complicated sound.

These photographs show the beautiful patterns that are produced by single, pure tones. Each tone is produced by a vibrating membrane. The vibrations are made visible by an oscilloscope,

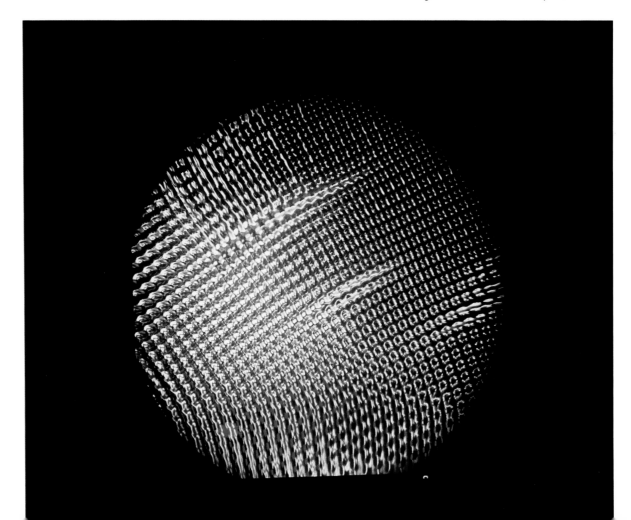

an electronic machine that detects vibrations and shows them as patterns on a television screen. The photograph is called an audioscope.

Sound waves, like water waves, come in different sizes, or amplitudes. They also come more or less often. How many occur in one second is called the frequency. The higher the frequency of a sound, the higher its pitch. Every pure tone has a single amplitude and a single frequency. A bass note has a large amplitude and a low frequency; a treble note has a small amplitude and a high frequency. In these audioscopes, the smaller pattern is made by the higher tone.

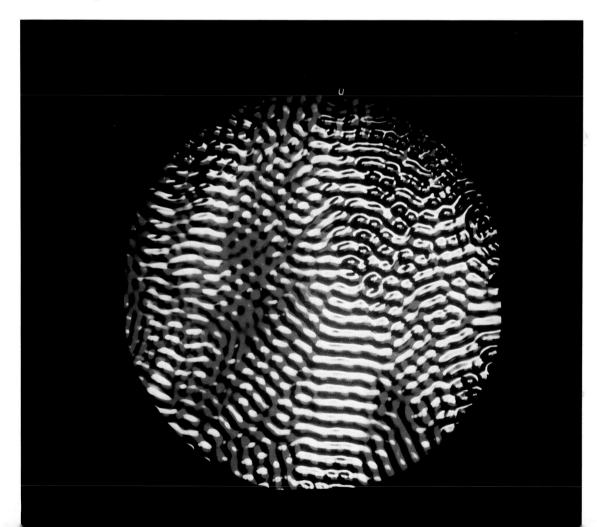

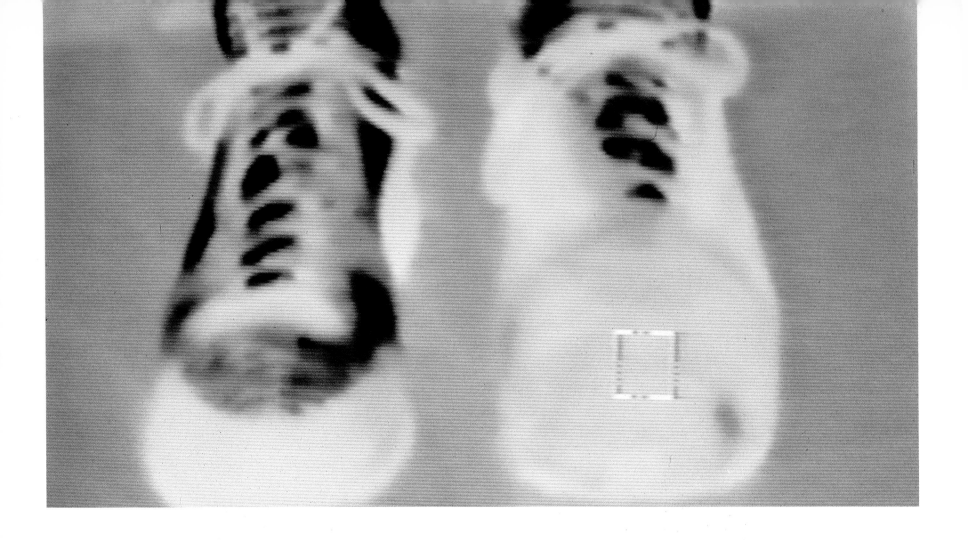

Running cool

Photographs are sometimes used to make the invisible visible. Thermography is a photographic technique for showing temperature differences as different colors. In the pictures on pages 20–21, sound is made visible; in these you can see heat. Hot feet may not be a fascinating subject to the average person, but they are of great interest to a running-shoe manufacturer. These thermograms compare running shoes to see which one keeps the runner's foot cooler.

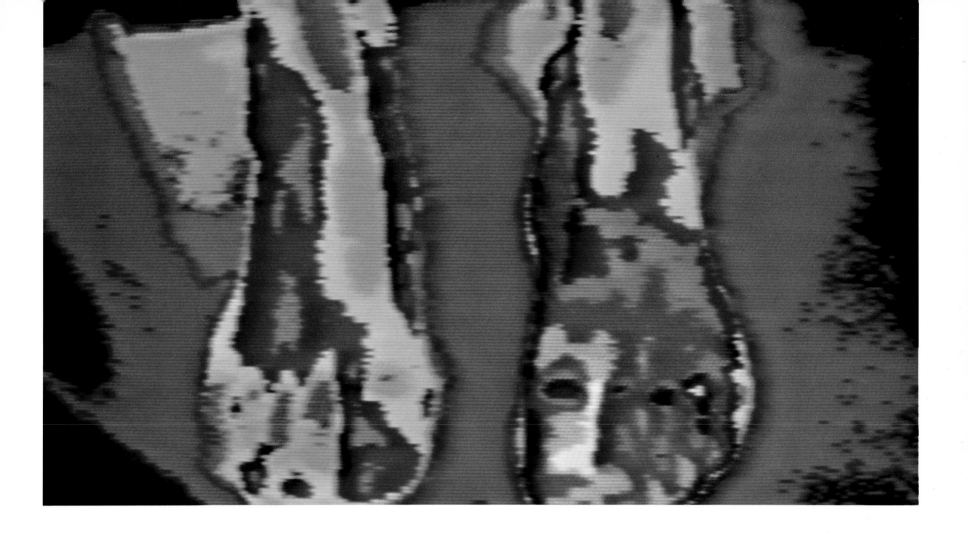

The black-and-white thermogram shows the feet of a runner, wearing two different types of test shoes, after five minutes of running. In this thermogram, white is hotter than black, so you can see that the foot at the right of the picture is hotter than the other foot. The color thermogram shows the runner's bare feet after five minutes of running in the test shoes. Purple, blue, and green are cooler than pink, red, and orange. Again, you can see that the foot on the right is hotter and that the ball of the foot gets hotter than the heels. If you were a runner, which shoe would you prefer?

INFRARED SKI SLOPE

To record images on film, ordinary photography uses light that the human eye can see. Some photographic film records light we can't see, such as X rays and infrared radiation. For taking pictures of the earth from the air, infrared photos have an advantage over ordinary photos: Infrared radiation cuts through the haze of the atmosphere to give a crisp, detailed photograph that might be blurry and indistinct if it were taken with ordinary color film.

This infrared photograph shows the ski area of Vail, Colorado. It was taken from inside a U-2 airplane at an altitude of 65,000 feet. It clearly shows the double ridge of mountains of the Gore Range of the Rocky Mountains. Warm areas of the trees give off more infrared radiation than the colder ski slopes, so infrared is particularly good for showing vegetation. Experts can use photos taken at altitudes lower than this one to tell sick trees from healthy ones. In this photo, the dark areas show healthy stands of pine and fir trees. On the right, running down the side of the picture, is Gore Creek. In the lower left-hand corner is the Beaver Creek ski area, which is about ten miles from Vail.

This kind of photo is often used in connection with computer-enhanced photos, taken from satellites, that survey the earth's crust. The infrared photos are like a *topographical map*, showing landmarks and the shape of the landscape. Mineral deposits may show up in the satellite photos. By comparing the two photos, the exact site of the mineral deposits can be located.

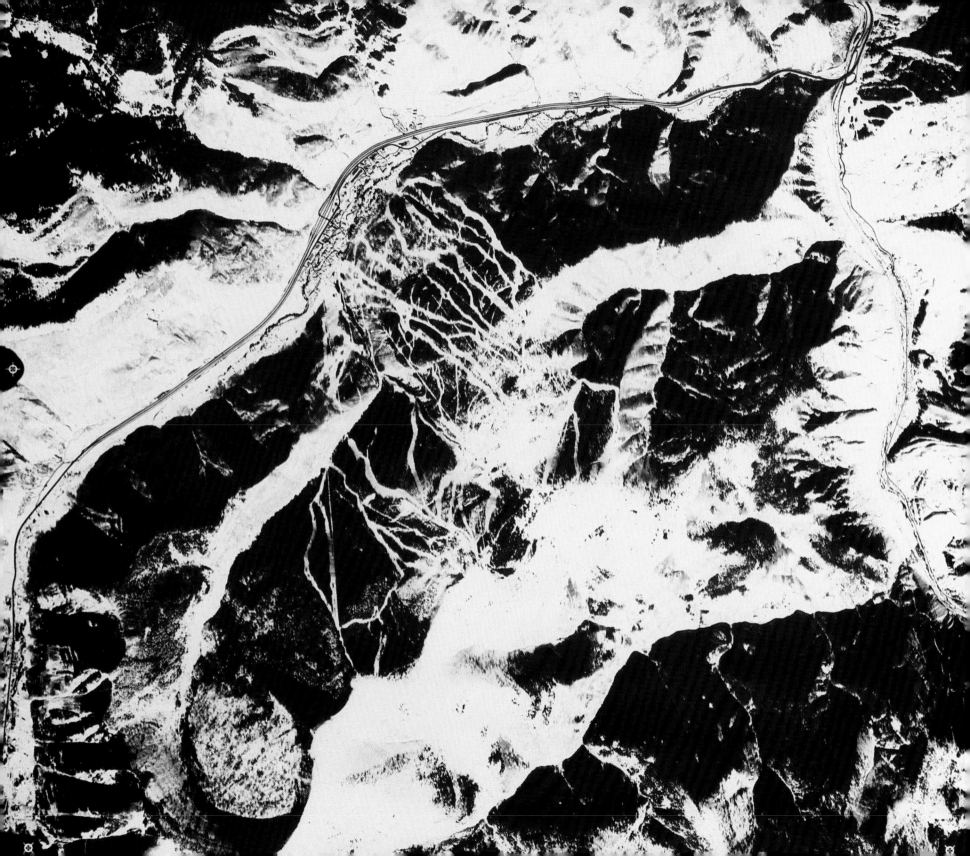

Popcorn

Popcorn is often the snack you eat when you're having fun. You've probably even done your share of popping. But it's very unlikely that you've seen a single kernel go through the stages of popping. It happens much too quickly. Now you can, thanks to this high-speed strobe photo. The trick in taking this picture was to trigger the camera when the popcorn popped, an unpredictable moment. The photographer, Greg Dale, invented a device to do just that. It is something like the electric eye that opens a door. Your body interrupts a beam of light, which sets off an electric signal that opens the door. Greg used a beam of infrared light that won't expose ordinary film. The setup was in total darkness and the camera shutter was left open. As the kernel started to pop, it moved up and broke the beam. That set off an electronic signal, tripping a strobe, which flashed every .02 seconds. This kernel took .1 seconds to pop. The exposed film showed five images.

Popcorn pops when the moisture inside the kernel becomes superheated steam. It develops a pressure of 135 pounds per square inch, which is nine times ordinary *atmospheric pressure*. The skin ruptures under the pressure, and the internal starch granules expand into thin, jellylike bubbles that fuse together and solidify. You can see a tiny jet of steam, propelling the kernel upward, emerging in the second image from the bottom. The droplets are hot oil forced into the air by the escaping steam. Notice that the skin of the kernel splits at one end and is rolled back much the way a banana skin is peeled.

There are often unpopped kernels in a bowl of microwave-popped corn. Next time you make some, see if you can find kernels that were in various stages of opening when the popping stopped. You can arrange them in order to show how the kernel expands when it pops. This photo can be a guide.

27

LISTENING TO WORDS AND MUSIC

How the brain works is an extraordinarily complicated mystery that has fascinated scientists for centuries. It is only in modern times that we have been able to develop a technology that reveals some of the brain's secrets, such as which parts of the brain are involved in interpreting language and perceiving music. The PET scan is an amazing medical diagnostic tool that can give a picture of the inside of the body, including the brain. Here's how it works.

A simple sugar, glucose, is injected into the bloodstream. It is exactly like the glucose in foods except that it is radioactive. The radioactivity is streams of tiny, electrically charged particles called positrons. The positrons are detected by positron emission tomography (PET for short). The PET scanning machine is like an X-ray machine. It shows very specific slices, or cross-sections, of the body. A PET scan shows where the radioactive glucose is absorbed by the body tissues.

These PET scans show a slice of the brain at the level of the eyes, as if you are looking down on it from above. The front of the head is the top of the images; the back of the head is at the bottom. The different colors show that the brain doesn't absorb the glucose evenly. On the right of the PET scan is a color band that shows the lowest amounts of glucose as deep blue (bottom) and the highest amounts as blue-white (top). The parts of the brain that are most stimulated take up the most glucose.

The red arrows indicate the areas of greatest glucose uptake when there is silence (the brain is resting) and when words and music, words alone, and music alone are heard.

AUDITORY STIMULATION

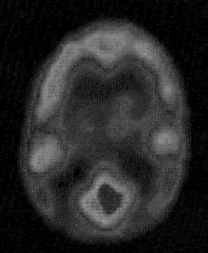

RESTING STATE

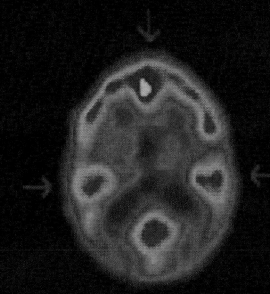

LANGUAGE AND MUSIC

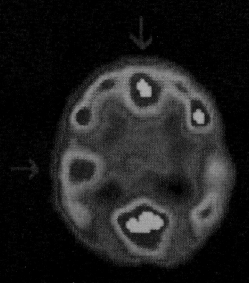

LANGUAGE

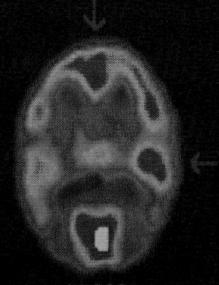

MUSIC

UCLA SCHOOL OF MEDICINE

PHELPS ET AL

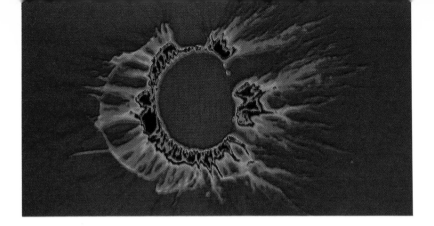

SCIENCE AND PLAY

Think of what you do when you play. You use your imagination. You try things out to see what will happen. You make up new rules. You pretend just for fun. Scientists do the same thing when they work. Sometimes when they're fooling around they make a discovery that can't be explained, that has no special use but is fun to think about.

Kirlian photographs detect a field of electricity that surrounds any living thing. The picture on this page was made by touching a fingertip to a plate that was coated with a material that was sensitive to the fingertip's extremely weak electrical force. The force was transformed into electronic signals, and the electronic information was put into a computer that enhanced the image by adding the brilliant color. Only living plants and animals give off this kind of electrical force.

Kirlian photography has not yet been put to work to further our understanding of nature. Electricity is involved in many life processes, such as nerve transmission and muscle contraction. Certain fish have senses that can detect electrical fields. Perhaps Kirlian photography could be useful to the scientists who study these phenomena. Perhaps electricity detection is the sixth sense. For the moment, Kirlian is a plaything of scientific photography. But now that you've seen it, when you say, "Let the force be with you," you know that the force is real.

GLOSSARY

altitude (AL-ti-tood) *Latin altitudo*, height, depth

The vertical elevation, or height, of an object above the ground or ocean surface.

atmosphere (AT-mo-sfear) *Greek atmos*, vapor + *Latin sphaera*, ball

The whole mass of air surrounding the earth. Atmospheric pressure is the pressure exerted by the earth's atmosphere at a given point on or above earth's surface.

counterbalance (KOWNT-er-bal-unts) *Latin contra*, against + *bi*, two + *lanx*, plate

A weight that balances or offsets another weight. In a phonograph tonearm, it is a moveable weight used to make sure the needle tracks smoothly and evenly in the grooves of the record.

enhancement (en-HAN-sment) *Latin in*, in or into + *altus*, high

An addition, contribution, or improvement. Computer enhancement is most often used to make an image clearer by making its parts more distinguishable.

fidelity (fi-DEL-it-ee) *Latin fidelis*, faithful

Exactness; the degree to which an electronic device, such as a phonograph or television, accurately reproduces sound or a picture.

gravity (GRAV-it-ee) *Latin gravis*, heavy

The force that attracts, or pulls, an object at the surface toward the center of a planet or other celestial body.

interval (IN-ter-vul) *Latin inter*, between + *vallum*, rampart, wall

A space between events, objects, units, or states. In music, the difference in pitch between tones.

mass (MAS) *Greek maza*, barley cake, and *massein*, to knead

The property of matter that causes a body to have weight in a gravitational field and is used as a measure of the amount of material the body contains.

momentum (mo-MEN-tum) *Latin momentum*, movement

The force of movement; the property of a body that determines how long it will take it to come to rest under a constant force.

tonearm (TOHN-arm) *Latin tonus*, tension + *Greek harmos*, joint

The movable part of a record player that carries the sound pickup unit and permits the needle to follow the record groove.

topography (top-OG-ra-fee) *Greek topos*, place + *graphein*, to write

Showing natural or man-made details of a place or region. A topographical map shows the relative positions and heights of features of the landscape.

INDEX

Italics indicate photographs.